OCTOBER

TIME-OUT TRIVIA

AN *ACTIVITY* FOR *EVERY DAY*

Written by Becky Daniel

Illustrated by Chris Nye

Good Apple

Executive Editor: Jeri Cipriano
Editor: Susan Eddy

GOOD APPLE
An Imprint of Modern Curriculum
A Division of Simon & Schuster
299 Jefferson Road, P.O. Box 480
Parsippany, NJ 07054-0480

ISBN: 1-56417-722-X

1 2 3 4 5 6 7 8 9   MAL   01 00 99 98 97 96

Table of Contents

To The Teacher

Each daily fact in this series of trivia books is based on historical and modern events designed to delight and motivate students and help them make important human connections with people who lived and accomplished interesting things many years ago or who still live and make a difference in our world today. People from other places will come alive for your students when they eagerly bite off another bit of daily trivia. For children who choose to take their learning a step further, a bonus activity is also found on each page.

Special October events include Fire Prevention Week, National Magic Week, World Poetry Day, Teddy Roosevelt's birthday, and many others. Activities include creating cartoon characters, tongue twisters, writing legends, estimating measurements, and much, much more.

You will know the very best way to present these activities in your classroom. But whether you use them as lesson extenders, in learning centers, or as daily sponge activities, children are certain to enjoy these engaging activities as they learn more about history. For your convenience, reproducible award certificates are included with this set of fun and educational trivia-based worksheets.

First Telephone Book

On October 1, 1785, John MacPherson published the first city directory in Philadelphia. The directory contained names and addresses of 6,250 citizens. MacPherson's directory was the forerunner of today's telephone book. Use the pages provided to create a personal telephone book. Write the names and numbers you know on the lines. (Put names in alphabetical order.) Then cut out the pages carefully. Cut a cover from construction paper the size of two of your telephone book pages placed side by side. Fold the cover in half, insert your directory pages, and staple. Personalize your cover in any way you choose.

Bonus: *In your personal telephone book, list names and numbers of at least twenty friends.*

A

Name _____

Address _____

_____

Phone _____

B

Name _____

Address _____

_____

Phone _____

C

Name _____

Address _____

_____

Phone _____

D

Name _____

Address _____

_____

Phone _____

E

Name _____

Address _____

_____

Phone _____

F

Name _____

Address _____

_____

Phone _____

G

Name _____

Address _____

_____

Phone _____

H

Name _____

Address _____

_____

Phone _____

I

Name _____

Address _____

_____

Phone _____

J

Name _____

Address _____

_____

Phone _____

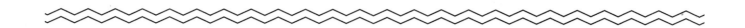

K

Name _____

Address _____

_____

Phone _____

L

Name _____

Address _____

_____

Phone _____

M

Name _____

Address _____

_____

Phone _____

N

Name _____

Address _____

_____

Phone _____

O

Name _____

Address _____

_____

Phone _____

P

Name _____

Address _____

_____

Phone _____

Q

Name _____

Address _____

_____

Phone _____

R

Name _____

Address _____

_____

Phone _____

S

Name _____

Address _____

_____

Phone _____

T

Name _____

Address _____

_____

Phone _____

U

Name   _____

Address _____

  _____

Phone   _____

V

Name   _____

Address _____

  _____

Phone   _____

W

Name   _____

Address _____

  _____

Phone   _____

X

Name   _____

Address _____

  _____

Phone   _____

Y

Name   _____

Address _____

  _____

Phone   _____

Z

Name   _____

Address _____

  _____

Phone   _____

NOTES

_____

_____

_____

_____

_____

_____

_____

_____

_____

_____

_____

_____

_____

_____

_____

_____

Model T Ford

On this date in 1908, the first Model T Ford was produced by the Ford Motor Company. Its original price of $850 was too high for the average family, so Henry Ford created the assembly-line method to reduce costs. This method utilized a conveyor belt to bring automobile parts to the workers. Each worker performed a certain task. The assembly line reduced the time it took to make a Model T from 12 1/2 worker hours to 1 1/2 worker hours. The car's cost dropped to $290, which made it affordable for the average family. In the chart below, compare the Model T Ford to the car your family owns. How are they the same? How are they different? Use your library to find out about the Model T.

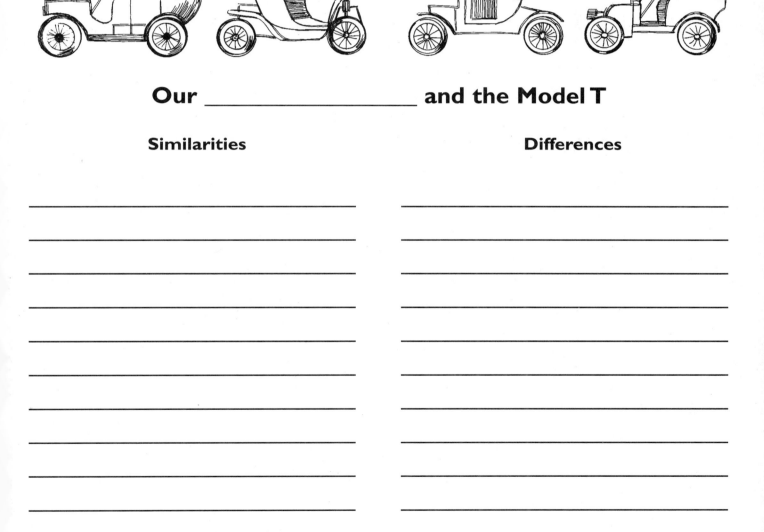

Our _____ and the Model T

Similarities	Differences
_____	_____
_____	_____
_____	_____
_____	_____
_____	_____
_____	_____
_____	_____
_____	_____
_____	_____
_____	_____

Bonus: *Try the assembly line method with a group of friends. Make submarine sandwiches two ways. First, have each person make an entire sandwich. Then share the sandwich-making by assigning each person a specific task, such as slicing the roll. See which way is the fastest way to produce a sandwich for everyone in the group.*

Happy Birthday, Snoopy

On this day in 1950, Charles M. Schulz's *Peanuts* comic strip appeared for the first time. *Peanuts* now appears in 2,300 newspapers and is translated into twenty-six languages. Can you draw a cartoon-type dog? Use the step-by-step directions below to make your own cartoon character.

Bonus: *Now that you can draw a dog, create a cartoon featuring your canine character. Don't forget to give your dog a name.*

First "Andy Griffith Show"

On this day in 1960, the first episode of the "Andy Griffith Show" was aired on television. Every year on this day, over 12,000 of the show's Rerun Watchers Club members celebrate. Do you belong to a fan club? If you created a new fan club, who would the club honor? Fill out the application for president of your new fan club below.

I, _____ ,
(NAME)

wish to be president of the

_____ Fan Club.

I will work hard to: _____

_____

_____

_____

Bonus: *List the names of three people who would like to be members of your fan club or write a fan letter to one of your favorite stars.*

Fire Prevention Week

The first or second week in October is set aside each year to increase people's awareness of fire safety. School programs teach children how to avoid starting fires and how to react when a fire breaks out. Think of one fire safety rule you have learned. Plan a skit which demonstrates the rule.

Fire Prevention Skit

By _____

_____

_____

_____

_____

_____

_____

_____

_____

_____

_____

_____

_____

_____

Bonus: *Get some friends to help you perform your skit for the class.*

International Balloon Festival

Albuquerque, New Mexico, is the site each year of the largest hot air balloon event in the world—the International Balloon Festival. It is one of the most photographed events in the United States. Hot air balloons come in a wide array of colors, shapes, and designs. Use a stamp pad, crayons, or markers to create interesting designs on the balloons below.

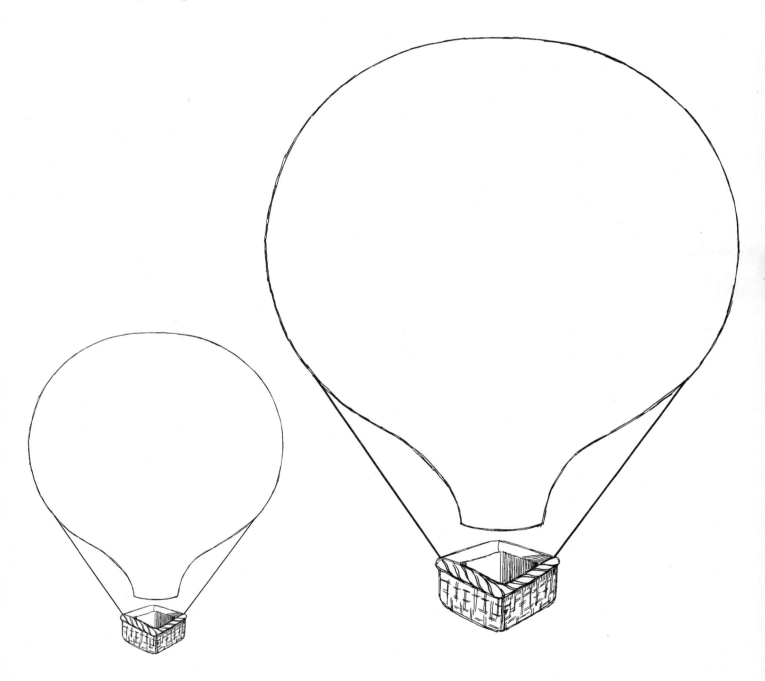

Bonus: *Cut out one balloon. Make a basket from construction paper and attach it to your balloon with colored ribbons. Hang it from your bedroom ceiling.*

Happy Birthday, American Library Association

On this day in 1876, the American Library Association was founded in Philadelphia, Pennsylvania. This association awards the Caldecott and Newbery medals for outstanding children's books. Find out what each medal stands for and look for former winners in your library. Then choose a book you have read and loved to receive each of the awards. Fill out an award certificate for each book. Explain in detail why the books were chosen.

AWESOME ILLUSTRATION AWARD CERTIFICATE

Awarded to _____

Illustrated by _____

I choose this book because _____

_____

_____

Name _____

Bonus: *Write a poem about books or reading.*

SUPER STORY
AWARD CERTIFICATE

Awarded to
_____

Written by
_____

I choose this book because
_____

_____

_____

Name
_____

Pickled Pepper Week

Have you ever tasted a bell, pimento, cherry, or chili pepper? Do you like hot, mild, or sweet pickled peppers? Once a year, Pickle Packers International, Inc., in St. Charles, Illinois, celebrates pickled peppers. Can you say the pickled pepper tongue twister without making a mistake? Practice it. Time yourself and see how many seconds it takes to say it three times without a mistake.

Peter Piper picked
a peck of pickled peppers.
A peck of pickled peppers
Peter Piper picked.
If Peter Piper picked
a peck of pickled papers,
How many pecks of pickled
peppers
did Peter Piper pick?

Bonus: *Write an original vegetable tongue twister.*

16

Great Chicago Fire

On this day in 1871, the Great Chicago Fire began. According to legend, the fire started when Mrs. O'Leary's cow kicked over a lantern in the barn. The fire killed 300 people and left 90,000 homeless. Because of this fire, the week that includes October 8 is designated Fire Prevention Week. Write a new legend telling how the Great Chicago Fire started or how it was put out.

The Great Chicago Fire

by _____

_____

_____

_____

_____

_____

_____

_____

_____

_____

_____

Bonus: *Draw a picture depicting your legend.*

National Metric Week

The week that includes October 10 is National Metric Week. The United States is the only major country that has not officially adopted the metric system. Estimate the measurements of the items listed below in both inches and centimeters. Then use an inch ruler or yardstick and a metric ruler or meter stick to measure the items. Do both the estimate and the actual measurement before proceeding to the next item. Were you better at making estimates in inches or centimeters? Did you get better as you went along?

	Prediction		Actual	
	Centimeters	Inches	Centimeters	Inches
1. your foot				
2. your right thumb				
3. your pencil				
4. your friend's nose				
5. distance from floor to top of your desk				
6. line under these words				
7. length of this paper				
8. your friend's shoe				

Bonus: *Find out how liters, meters, and grams are related and explain it in one paragraph. Use pictures if it will help you.*

Celebrate Foods

Autumn weekends are for celebrating many different kinds of food. Food happenings around the nation in early October include a clam chowderfest in Mystic, Connecticut; chili cook-offs in Texas; an oyster festival on Chincoteague Island, Virginia; the Vermont Apple Festival; the West Virginia Grape Growers Meeting; and the South Carolina Sweet Potato Festival. Plan a weekend celebration of your favorite food. Name the celebration and plan the activities.

Bonus: *Collect three recipes that use the food you are celebrating or create three new recipes using that food.*

Ferris Wheel

On this date in 1893, the World's Columbian Exposition in Chicago, Illinois, closed—but not before its main feature, a "pleasure wheel" built by George Washington Gale Ferris, took 2.5 million people for a ride. The 2,807,498-pound wheel, which stood more than 250-feet tall, carried 2,160 persons on each 40-minute ride. They rode in 36 streetcar-sized cages. Today, these pleasure wheels are known as Ferris wheels in honor of their inventor. Invent a new amusement park ride suitable for people of all ages. Draw it in the space below and give it a name.

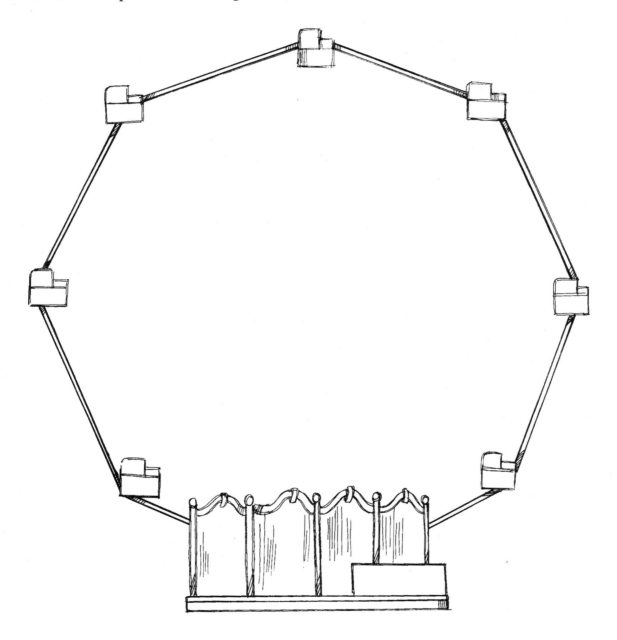

Bonus: *What is your favorite amusement park ride? Describe it in a paragraph without using its name. Read your paragraph to the class and see if anyone can guess what you are describing.*

October 12
Columbus Day

Columbus Day, celebrated on the second Monday in October, commemorates the anniversary of Christopher Columbus's first landing on San Salvador, an island off the coast of the United States, on October 12, 1492. How many words can you find in "Christopher Columbus?" The letters must appear in order but they do not have to be right next to each other. For example, you can spell the word *tub*.

CHRISTOPHER COLUMBUS

1. tub _____
2. _____
3. _____
4. _____
5. _____
6. _____
7. _____
8. _____
9. _____
10. _____
11. _____
12. _____
13. _____

14. _____
15. _____
16. _____
17. _____
18. _____
19. _____
20. _____
21. _____
22. _____
23. _____
24. _____
25. _____

Bonus: *Give yourself one point for each three-letter word, two points for each four-letter word, and five points for any longer words. What is your score? Compare your score to a friend's.*

White House

On this date in 1792, the cornerstone for the White House was laid. The White House is the official residence of the President of the United States and one of the most popular tourist attractions in the country. The White House had no electricity for more than one hundred years after it was built. Its interior has been renovated and redecorated many times. Pretend you are the President of the United States. In the space below, design a floor plan of a room that would meet the needs of you and your family if you were living in the White House.

Bonus: *Find out the name of the man who won the contest to design the White House. Can you find out who was the first baby born in the White House?*

National School Lunch Week

Presidential proclamation has decreed that National School Lunch Week begins on the second Sunday in October. Pretend it is your job to plan the school lunches for one week. What will be on your school lunch menu?

MONDAY		TUESDAY
_____	**M**	_____
_____	**e**	_____
_____	**n**	_____
_____	**u**	_____
_____		_____
_____		_____
_____		_____
_____		_____

Bonus: *Choose something from the regular school lunch menu you really like and write a note to the cafeteria staff complimenting them on it.*

WEDNESDAY

_____

_____

_____

_____

_____

_____

_____

_____

_____

_____

THURSDAY

_____

_____

_____

_____

_____

_____

_____

_____

_____

_____

Menu

FRIDAY

_____

_____

_____

_____

_____

_____

_____

_____

_____

_____

Hooray for Desserts

Each year, National Dessert Day is celebrated in New York City. What is your favorite dessert? Is it pudding, ice cream, fruit, pie, or cake? Draw and color a picture of your favorite dessert.

My Favorite Dessert

By _____

Bonus: *List ten adjectives that describe your favorite dessert.*

World Poetry Day

Today is World Poetry Day—a day set aside to discover new poems and enjoy old favorites. Do you have a favorite poem? (Remember that song lyrics are poems first—before the melodies are added.) Copy your favorite poem or lyrics below. Be sure to include the name of the poet.

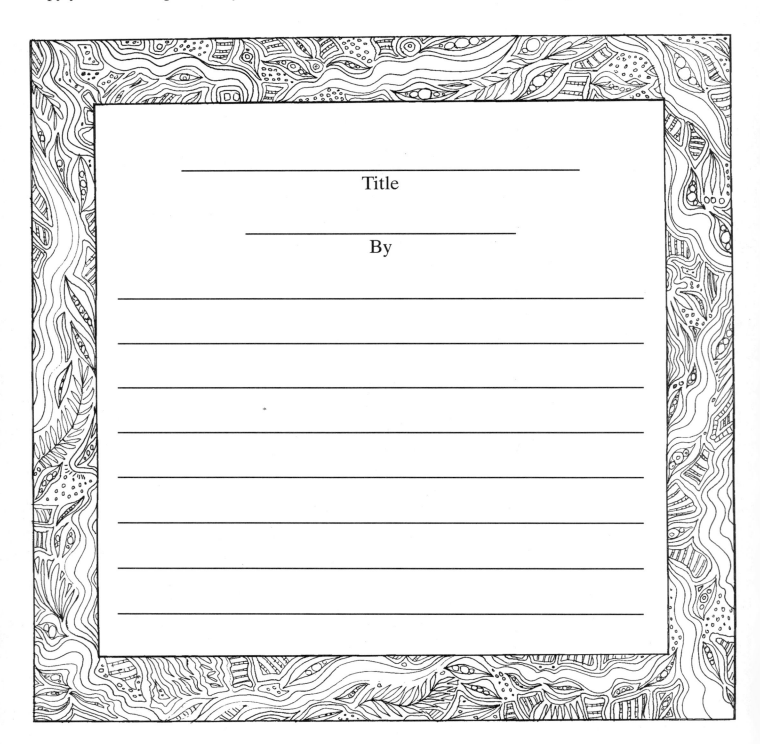

_____
Title

_____
By

_____

_____

_____

_____

_____

_____

_____

Bonus: *Ask someone in your home to read you their favorite poem.*

October 16
Happy Birthday, Noah Webster

Noah Webster—lawyer, teacher, editor, and author of Webster's Dictionary—was born on this date in l758. He published his first dictionary in 1806. Celebrate Webster's birthday by using a dictionary to answer these questions:

egress • catacomb • crimsom • aplomb

USING THE DICTIONARY

1. Would you find an <u>egress</u> in the zoo? —————

2. Would you groom pets with <u>catacombs</u>?

   ————

3. Would you find a <u>conch</u> in a living room or on

   a beach? ——————

4. What are three meanings of the word <u>kid</u>?

   ————   ————   ————

5. Is <u>crimson</u> a kind of boat or a color? —————

6. Which letter is silent in the word <u>aplomb</u>?

   ——————

egress • catacomb • crimsom • aplomb

Bonus: *Create your own dictionary questions to stump a friend.*

Lunch Break?

On October 17, 1977, at the Donut Shop in Reedley, California, Peter Dowdeswell ate forty jam and butter sandwiches in less than 18 minutes. His record has since been broken. If you were trying to set a record for eating, what food would you choose to eat? Draw a picture of yourself eating that food below. Tell how much you could eat in 20 minutes.

Bonus: *Look in the* Guinness Book of World Records *to find out about other food records.*

Alaska Day

Today is the anniversary of the day the United States purchased Alaska from Russia for $7,200,000 in 1867. Alaska remained a U.S. territory until 1959, when both Alaska and Hawaii became states. The American flag had to be changed to include the two extra stars. Pretend we are getting another new state. What might it be? Design an American flag with 51 stars.

Bonus: *Look in an atlas or other reference to see what each state flag looks like. Then design a flag for your new state.*

Oktoberfest

In nearly every state in the United States, Oktoberfest celebrations take place this month. In Germany, Oktoberfest is a 16-day celebration which ends the first Sunday in October. It originated there in 1810 to celebrate the wedding of a king and queen. These days it is simply a reason for fun. Oktoberfest celebrations in the United States often include folk dancing, harvest foods, and craft shows. Notice how the German words *Oktober* and *Fest* were combined to make the new word *Oktoberfest*. Create a new holiday by combining the name of a month with another word. Tell how your holiday is celebrated today.

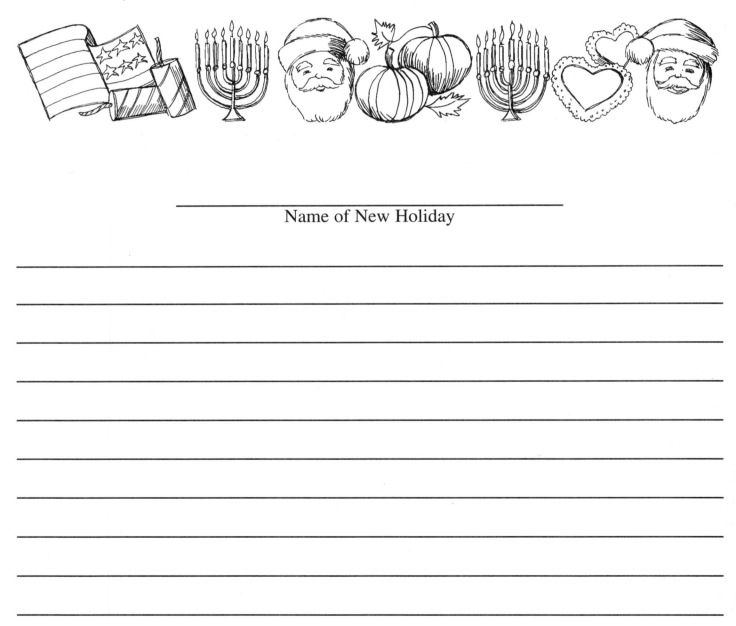

_____
Name of New Holiday

_____

_____

_____

_____

_____

_____

_____

_____

Bonus: *Write a paragraph about your made-up holiday to tell how it first came to be.*

National Cleaner Air Week

The last full week in October is set aside to remind people not to pollute the air. Pretend you have permission to paint a mural depicting the importance of clean air. What message would you try to convey? Plan your mural in the space below.

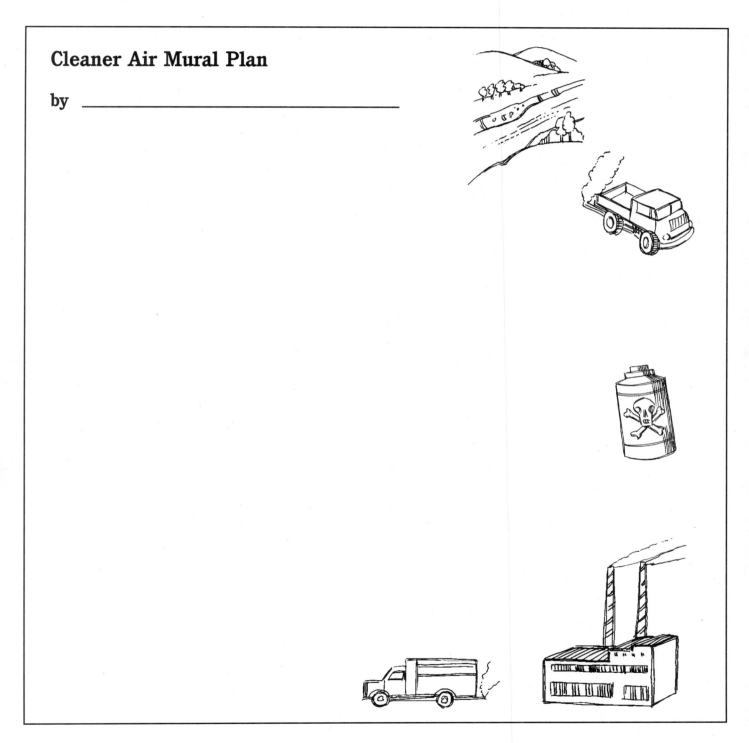

Cleaner Air Mural Plan

by _____

Bonus: *Ask your principal or teacher for space in the hall to display your cleaner air mural.*

End of Hurricane Season

If you live in the Virgin Islands, today is a legal holiday celebrating the end of the hurricane season. Hurricane season lasts from June to October. Look at the word hurricane and find the smaller word that means "a walking aid." Like the word *cane*, many small words can be found within larger words. Below are a few word-within-word challenges for you. How many can you guess? Each answer includes the big word as well as the little word within it. Unscramble the letters to the big words to get your answers.

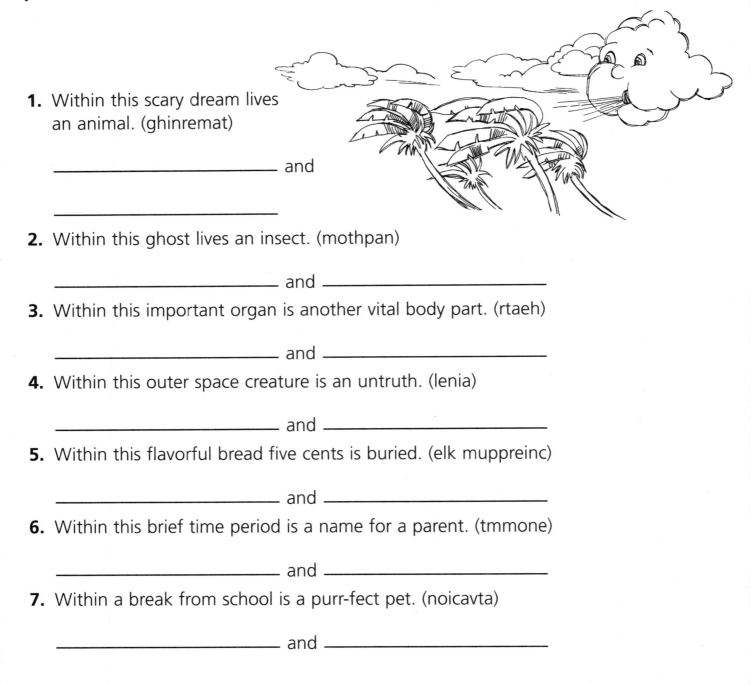

1. Within this scary dream lives an animal. (ghinremat)

_____ and

_____

2. Within this ghost lives an insect. (mothpan)

_____ and _____

3. Within this important organ is another vital body part. (rtaeh)

_____ and _____

4. Within this outer space creature is an untruth. (lenia)

_____ and _____

5. Within this flavorful bread five cents is buried. (elk muppreinc)

_____ and _____

6. Within this brief time period is a name for a parent. (tmmone)

_____ and _____

7. Within a break from school is a purr-fect pet. (noicavta)

_____ and _____

Bonus: *Create your own word-within-word challenges.*

Parachute Jump

On October 22, 1797, Andre Jacques Garnerin made the first successful parachute jump from a hot-air balloon at Monçeau Park in Paris. He jumped from an altitude of 3,000 feet. What do you think it would feel like to jump out of a balloon and float down to Earth? What do you think it would be like to pull a cord and see a parachute open above your head? Follow these directions to make a parachute.

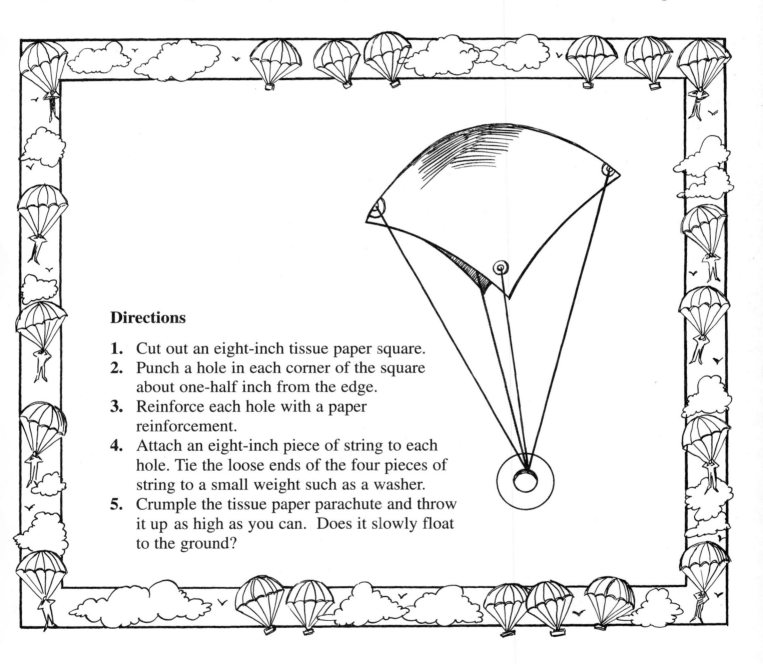

Directions

1. Cut out an eight-inch tissue paper square.
2. Punch a hole in each corner of the square about one-half inch from the edge.
3. Reinforce each hole with a paper reinforcement.
4. Attach an eight-inch piece of string to each hole. Tie the loose ends of the four pieces of string to a small weight such as a washer.
5. Crumple the tissue paper parachute and throw it up as high as you can. Does it slowly float to the ground?

Bonus: *Try some variations of this activity. Instead of crumpling the tissue, try folding it in different ways. Try making parachutes from different materials and varying the weights or the size of the parachute. Decide which one works the best.*

Swallows Leave San Juan Capistrano

Today is traditionally the day that the swallows depart from the old mission in San Juan Capistrano, California, and fly south for the winter. How do birds know that it is October 23? How do they know how to fly in a certain direction? Pretend that one San Juan Capistrano bird doesn't have a "built-in" calendar or compass. Suppose *he* must travel by bus. Use the postcard below to write a note from this mixed-up swallow who is on his way south.

Bonus: *Draw a cartoon with a caption about your imaginary swallow.*

October 24
United Nations Day

The United Nations is a world organization that seeks to accomplish two goals—world peace and world security. The organization promotes good relations and cooperation among nations as a way to achieve these goals. You can start a correspondence with a boy or girl from another country by sending a self-addressed stamped envelope to: *International Friendship League, Inc.*, 40 Mount Vernon Street, Boston, MA 02108. They will send you an application. Write your letter to the International Friendship League below.

Bonus: *Do research to find out what United Nations agencies such as UNICEF and UNESCO do around the world.*

National Magic Week

The last week in October is set aside to demonstrate friendship and companionship through magic shows at hospitals and nursing homes in America. Here is a magic number trick you can show your family and friends. You will need the Magic Numbers Card found on the next page. Close your eyes. Ask a person to point to a number on the card without telling or showing you the number. Then ask that person to tell you the letter above each column in which that number appears. For example, if the number is 10, your friend will say that the secret number is in columns B and D. Open your eyes. To discover the secret number, you simply add together the numbers in the top row of the columns that contain the secret number (2 + 8 = 10). Try this trick with lots of numbers and you will see that it always works. (If you memorize the first row numbers, you can do the whole trick without opening your eyes!) Cut out the Magic Numbers Card and glue it to a piece of construction paper or oaktag. Show the trick to at least three people today.

Bonus: *Show your magic number trick to someone home in bed, in a hospital, or in a nursing home.*

A	B	C	D
1	2	4	8
3	3	5	9
5	6	6	10
7	7	7	11
9	10	12	12
11	11	13	13
13	14	14	14
15	15	15	15

Mule Day

On October 26, 1785, King Charles III of Spain gave the United States a pair of mules as a gift. It is said that George Washington bred the first mules born in this country. A mule is the offspring of a female horse and a male donkey. Its horse mother gives it a large, well-shaped body, strong muscles, and its adaptability to a harness. From its donkey father, a mule gets its endurance and sure-footedness as well as its braying sound. Mules are strong, hardy workers. Choose two animals to be parents of a new species of animal. Draw a picture of their offspring and describe the qualities and characteristics it inherits from each parent.

Name of animal   Name of animal

Bonus: *What do you get when you cross a computer with a kangaroo? A computer that jumps to conclusions! Just for fun, make up crazy animal riddles.*

Happy Birthday, Teddy Roosevelt

Theodore Roosevelt was born on this day in 1858 and became President of the United States when he was only 42 years old. The teddy bear became associated with President Roosevelt as a result of a hunting trip in Mississippi. Some members of the hunting party caught a little brown bear cub. Teddy Roosevelt forced them to let it go free. The story appeared in many newspapers and toymakers were inspired to design a toy bear which came to be known as a teddy bear. What was your favorite stuffed animal? On the lines below, write what it would say if it suddenly came to life.

Bonus: *Read about Teddy Roosevelt. Find out why he is considered the first environmental president.*

Great Pumpkin Festivals

Many states have pumpkin festivals at this time of year. Pumpkin carving, painting jack-o'-lanterns, costume parades, and pumpkin recipes are often part of these celebrations. Think of a new game or activity for a pumpkin festival, such as Pin the Nose on the Pumpkin. Describe your activity below.

Bonus: *Create a menu of all-pumpkin treats, including such things as pumpkin salad dressing and pumpkin ice cream. Can you come up with enough ideas for breakfast, lunch, and dinner meals?*

Statue of Liberty

The Statue of Liberty was dedicated on this day in 1886. Frederic-Auguste Bartholdi created the famous sculpture as a gift from the people of France to the United States on the 100th anniversary of American independence. Construction problems delayed its arrival. If you were asked to sculpt a statue representing our country, what shape would it take? Draw a figure below that represents your feelings for America.

Bonus: *Carve your figure from soap or sculpt it from clay.*

Limousine Scavenger Hunt

In Tacoma, Washington, on the Thursday before Halloween people in costumes form teams and go on a scavenger hunt, traveling in *limousines!* You don't need a limousine to go on a word scavenger hunt. The scrambled words represent items you might search for on a scavenger hunt. See how many you can unscramble.

1. flea _____

2. tones _____

3. slleh _____

4. nabe _____

5. pepar plic _____

6. reeftha _____

7. kobo _____

8. berrub adnb _____

9. hotpogaphr _____

10. wolfre _____

11. danyc wepparr _____

12. noodew loops _____

13. geg lhesl _____

14. calstip rofk _____

15. cinpel _____

16. tarorc _____

Bonus: *See how many of these things you can find at home or near your home. Put them in a paper bag and bring them to school.*

The War of the Worlds

On this day in 1938, Orson Welles' radio play, "The War of the Worlds," was broadcast. The play was so real that many listeners believed Martians had truly invaded New Jersey. Today, we know there is no life on Mars. But some people believe there may be intelligent life on other planets. If you could send a message by space capsule to another planet, what would you want to say? Use pictures and symbols to convey your message. (Aliens don't speak English!)

Bonus: *Show your message to friends and see if they understand the message.*

Halloween

Halloween dates back to "All Hallow's Eve," a pagan custom honoring the sun god for the harvest. The wearing of costumes can be traced back to Celtic tradition. People dressed as saints and angels and paraded through churchyards to scare away evil creatures or roving souls which might be looking for bodies to inhabit. Today, Halloween is just a fun time and a reason to wear costumes and go trick-or-treating. You can use any of the patterns found on the following pages to decorate a paper plate and create a mask. Use paints, crayons, or markers to color your mask. Add yarn ties to hold it on or attach a stick at the bottom for holding your mask in front of your face.

Bonus: *Use a large plastic trash bag to create a costume to go with your mask.*

45

Answer Key

1. bus
2. comb
3. combs
4. crop
5. crops
6. crumb
7. crumbs
8. elm
9. elms
10. her
11. herb
12. herbs
13. hop
14. hops
15. hip
16. hips
17. his
18. hub
19. hubs
20. hum
21. hums
22. I
23. is
24. it
25. its
26. rip
27. rips
28. rope
29. ropes
30. rob
31. robs
32. rub
33. rubs
34. sob
35. sobs
36. stop
37. stops
38. sum
39. sums
40. the
41. to
42. tomb
43. tombs
44. too
45. tool
46. tools
47. top
48. tops
49. tub
50. tubs
51. us

1. No; an *egress* is an exit.
2. No; *catacombs* are underground rooms in which ancient people buried their dead.
3. At the beach; a *conch* is a sea mollusk or its shell.
4. A young goat; a child; to tease or fool.
5. A color; crimson is a shade of red.
6. The letter *b* is silent in the word *aplomb.*

1. nightmare/mare
2. phantom/ant
3. heart/ear
4. alien/lie
5. pumpernickel/nickel
6. moment/mom
7. vacation/cat

Bonus: Teddy Roosevelt loved camping and exploring the wilderness and established National Parks' protected areas.

1. leaf
2. stone
3. shell
4. bean
5. paper clip
6. feather
7. book
8. rubber band
9. photograph
10. flower
11. candy wrapper
12. wooden spool
13. egg shell
14. plastic fork
15. pencil
16. carrot

October Trivia Superstar

_____   _____
Awarded to   Date

_____
Signed

You're Tops at Trivia!

_____   _____
Awarded to   Date

_____
Signed